MAJ

Picture the Past
Life on a PIONEER HOMESTEAD

Sally Senzell Isaacs

Heinemann Library
Chicago, Illinois

© 2001 Reed Educational & Professional Publishing
Published by Heinemann Library,
an imprint of Reed Educational & Professional Publishing,
100 N. LaSalle, Suite 1010
Chicago, IL 60602
Customer Service 888-454-2279
Visit our website at www.heinemannlibrary.com

Produced for Heinemann Library by
    Bender Richardson White.
Editor: Lionel Bender
Designer: Ben White
Picture Researcher: Cathy Stastny
Media Conversion and Typesetting: MW Graphics
Production Controller: Kim Richardson

04 03 02 01
10 9 8 7 6 5 4 3 2 1

Printed in Hong Kong

Library of Congress Cataloging-in-Publication Data.
Issacs, Sally Senzell, 1950-
    Life on a pioneer homestead / Sally Senzell Isaacs.
        p. cm. – (Picture the past)
    Includes bibliographical references and index.
    Summary: An overview of life on a pioneer homestead including building a home, cooking food, clothing, schools, and everyday activities.

ISBN 1-57572-313-1 (library binding)
1. Frontier and pioneer life-United States-Juvenile literature. 2. United States-Social life and customs-1783-1865-Juvenile literature.
(1. Frontier and pioneer life. 2. United States-Social life and customs-1783-1865.) I. Title.

E179.5 .I83 2000
973.5-dc21
                                99-089883
Special thanks to Mike Carpenter, Scott Westerfield, and Tristan Boyer Binns at Heinemann Library for editorial and design guidance and direction.

Acknowledgments
The producers and publishers are grateful to the following for permission to reproduce copyright material: The Bridgeman Art Library: Museum of the City of New York, page 21; Private Collection, page 24. Corbis: Scott T. Smith, page 10; Robert Holmes, page 11; Wolfgang Kaehler, page 13; Annie Griffiths Bett, page 18; Richard T. Nowitz, page 20. Peter Newark's American Pictures, pages 3, 14, 15, 16, 25, 26, 27, 28. North Wind Pictures, pages 1, 6, 8, 19, 23.
Cover photograph: Peter Newark's American Pictures.

Every effort has been made to contact copyright holders of any material reproduced in this book. Omissions will be rectified in subsequent printings if notice is given to the publisher.

Illustrations by John James, pages 12, 17, 22; Gerald Wood, pages 7, 9; James Field, page 30.
Maps: Stefan Chabluk.
Cover make-up: Mike Pilley, Pelican Graphics.

Note to the Reader
Some words are shown in bold, **like this**.
You can find out what they mean by looking in the glossary.

ABOUT THIS BOOK

This book tells about pioneer life from around 1780 to 1850. Pioneers were the first people to move from the eastern United States to the western parts. They wanted to set up and own homesteads. A homestead was a house with open land all around.

We have illustrated the book with paintings from those times and with artists' ideas of how things looked then. We have included historic photographs that show life on the homesteads. Modern photographs show people dressed as pioneers and buildings that remain from pioneer times.

The Consultant
Special thanks go to Diane Smolinski for her help in the preparation of this series. Diane Smolinski has years of experience interpreting standards documents and putting them into practice.

The Author
Sally Senzell Isaacs is a professional writer and editor of nonfiction books for children. She graduated from Indiana University, earning a B.S. degree in Education with majors in American History and Sociology. For some years, she was the Editorial Director of Reader's Digest Educational Division. Sally Senzell Isaacs lives in New Jersey with her husband and two children.

CONTENTS

Settling in New Land

Many pioneers were people who left their homes in Virginia and North Carolina and traveled to the other side of the Appalachian Mountains. These pioneers settled in the woods and along the rivers and streams of Kentucky and Tennessee. Native Americans lived on this land long before the pioneers ever heard of it.

When the pioneers first arrived, they built small **cabins** and planted small fields. Over the years, they built bigger homes and planted bigger fields.

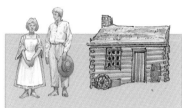

LOOK FOR THESE
The illustration of a pioneer boy and girl sits alongside the title of each double-page story in the book.

The picture of a pioneer house marks boxes with interesting facts about **homestead** life.

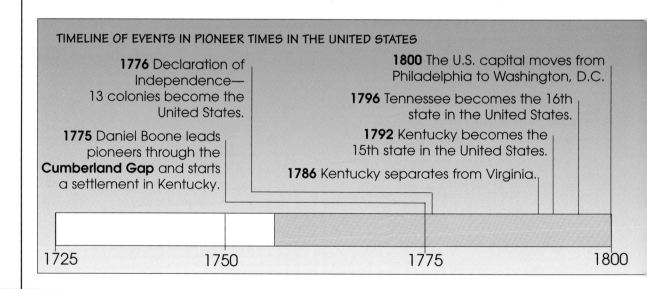

TIMELINE OF EVENTS IN PIONEER TIMES IN THE UNITED STATES

1776 Declaration of Independence— 13 colonies become the United States.

1775 Daniel Boone leads pioneers through the **Cumberland Gap** and starts a settlement in Kentucky.

1800 The U.S. capital moves from Philadelphia to Washington, D.C.

1796 Tennessee becomes the 16th state in the United States.

1792 Kentucky becomes the 15th state in the United States.

1786 Kentucky separates from Virginia.

1725   1750   1775   1800

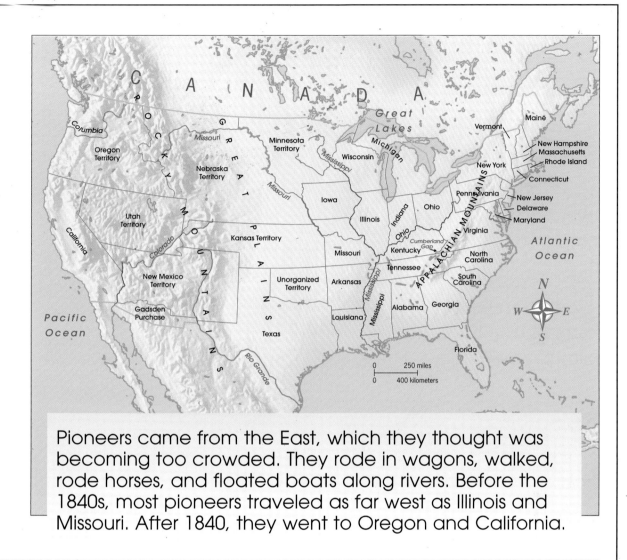

Pioneers came from the East, which they thought was becoming too crowded. They rode in wagons, walked, rode horses, and floated boats along rivers. Before the 1840s, most pioneers traveled as far west as Illinois and Missouri. After 1840, they went to Oregon and California.

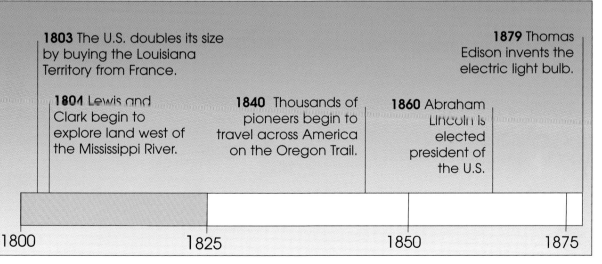

1803 The U.S. doubles its size by buying the Louisiana Territory from France.

1804 Lewis and Clark begin to explore land west of the Mississippi River.

1840 Thousands of pioneers begin to travel across America on the Oregon Trail.

1860 Abraham Lincoln is elected president of the U.S.

1879 Thomas Edison invents the electric light bulb.

1800   1825   1850   1875

On the Move

It was not easy to be a pioneer. Pioneers left most things behind them to travel into unknown land. Mothers, fathers, children, and grandparents traveled together. Some pioneers rode but most walked—for many weeks. They walked through the **Cumberland Gap** that led through the mountains into Kentucky and Tennessee.

Every night, the pioneers stopped, built a fire, and cooked a quick meal of corn bread and dried beef. They slept on the ground.

This family is traveling west on the Ohio River. When they get to their new land, they will use the wood from the boat to build a **shelter**.

The pioneers packed their belongings on their horses and cows, or on their wagons, carts, or boats. They brought only a few important things. Most people brought a cooking pot, an ax, some blankets, a sack of seeds, and a bag of corn meal. Children brought a few toys and games to play with.

NEWS REPORTS

People in the East read about pioneers in newspapers and in letters from pioneer relatives. Travelers also brought back stories about the pioneers and Native Americans.

Building a Home

Many pioneers chose land near a lake or stream. They needed water for drinking, cooking, and washing. The new land was covered with trees. The pioneers chopped the trees to make room for their fields and their houses. They used the trees to build the houses.

Neighbors helped each other to clear out rocks, chop trees, move logs, and build the **cabins**.

FORCED OUT

Pioneers and Native Americans usually got along. At times there was fighting. Finally, the pioneers forced almost all the Native Americans to move away and go farther west.

It took almost 80 trees to make one small cabin. Pioneers cut the trees into long logs. They cut **notches** in both ends of a log so that one log fit on top of another. To keep out the rain and wind, they stuffed leaves and mud between the logs. The roofs were usually made of large sheets of **canvas** that were waterproofed by painting them with plant oils.

Inside a Cabin

The first **cabins** had just one room measuring about 16 feet wide and 20 feet long (about 5 by 6 meters). The most important part of the room was the fireplace. Pioneers had no glass for the windows. They put oil on paper and hung it over the window to let in some light.

This cabin has one room. The toilet is outside in a smaller wooden house called an outhouse.

The family used the fireplace for cooking, warmth, and light. The cabin floor was made with split logs.

Pioneers started out with no furniture. They built wooden benches, chairs, and a table. Later they may have bought a metal bed frame from a store back east. They made mattresses by hand out of straw or corn **husks**. Some children climbed a ladder to a sleeping **loft** near the roof.

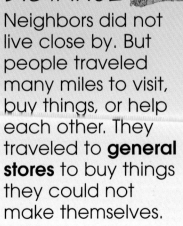

LONG DISTANCE
Neighbors did not live close by. But people traveled many miles to visit, buy things, or help each other. They traveled to **general stores** to buy things they could not make themselves.

A Grown-Up's Day

Pioneers had to make almost everything. Men made wooden plates for eating and beds for sleeping. Women made soap, candles, quilts, and clothes. Each job took many hours. Children helped their mothers and fathers.

The father chops wood. He uses some wood for the fire and some to make toys for his children.

Electric lights had not been invented yet. Pioneers burned candles every night. They made candles by dipping a bundle of twisted fibers into hot wax many times.

Vegetables had to be planted in the spring and picked in the fall. Wood had to be chopped for the fire. Every day someone carried buckets of water from the stream or **well** to the house. Cows had to be milked and chickens fed. Pioneers hunted and fished for their family's meals.

GARDEN MEDICINE

There were few doctors. Pioneer women took care of sick people. They used plants, roots, and flowers to cure most illnesses.

Pioneer Children

Children had to work hard. They went to the woods and gathered nuts and berries for cooking. Young children stood in the field and shouted at birds that tried to eat the corn. As children grew, they learned how to hunt, chop wood, and make clothes. They were taught how to carve wood with a knife to make a toy boat, doll, or whistle.

Grandparents, parents, and children lived together on the **homestead**. Children did not leave home until they got married.

Children always found time to play. They played tag and hide-and-seek. They had a tug-of-war with a strong rope. Their toys were not fancy. To make a ball, they wrapped scraps of yarn around a stone. They used tree vines to make a jump rope.

This boy and girl play on their father's hay wagon as it is brought in from the field.

School

As soon as many **homesteads** were set up, pioneers built schools. Children walked many miles to get to the school. Some schools were open only two or three months in the winter. In the fall, spring, and summer children had to help on the farm.

The school was usually just a one-room **cabin** with rows of desks. Here is a woman teacher and her students outside their school.

A wood-burning stove kept the classroom warm. The only light came through the windows. Students were in charge of cleaning the school. They swept the floors and carried water from the **well** or stream.

One teacher taught all the children in the school. The teacher lived with the students' families, moving from one house to another.

School Lessons

Everyone learned reading, writing, and **arithmetic**. Usually, students wrote on paper with a sharpened end of a feather. They dipped the feather in ink. There was usually just one book for the class to share. Each student read a few lines and passed the book to the next student.

Paper cost a lot of money. Some students wrote on black **slates** using white chalk. They could wipe their slates clean with a cloth.

Children were called to the front of the class to act out stories.

WRITING RIGHT

Some students preferred to write with their left hands. But teachers did not allow that. Everyone was forced to be right-handed.

The were many school rules. Students were punished for arriving late. They were punished for answering questions incorrectly or for falling asleep in class. Teachers made students write the same sentence over and over again. Or, they made students sit in a corner and wear a **dunce cap**.

Clothes

Pioneers had only one or two things to wear. They wore them over and over again. Girls and women always wore long dresses and **aprons**. Men and boys wore pants of wool or deer skin. Many people went barefoot in the summer. This kept their shoes from wearing out.

This woman uses a spinning wheel to turn sheep's wool into yarn.

Women made all the clothes. First they **sheared** the wool from their sheep. They put this wool on a spinning wheel to make yarn. They used a **loom** to weave the yarn into cloth. They sewed the cloth into dresses, shirts, and pants.

REUSE CLOTH

When a dress or shirt was worn out, pioneers cut up the cloth to make a
• rag doll
• quilt
• rag rug
• patches for a pair of torn pants

Many women wore hats all day. Many pioneers came from other countries, such as Germany, Sweden, Holland, Scotland, and Ireland, and brought with them fashions from their homeland.

Buying Things

After many families moved to an area, someone would open a **general store**. Instead of making everything, now pioneers could buy some things. The general store sold boots, hats, seeds, tools, flour, sugar, cotton and linen cloth, and medicine. These goods were delivered to the store by horses and horse-drawn wagons.

The general store was the center for buying, selling, and trading. One man is trading with a Native American.

People also went to the general store for news. One customer would report about a new baby or a lost horse. The store owner would spread the news to the next customers. Everyone's mail was delivered to the general store. So was a newspaper from the closest city.

Some people lived too far from the general store. They bought things from a traveling salesman.

Having Fun

Neighbors got together to build barns, fences, houses, and schools. Some people traveled for days on foot or on horseback to join a work party. They brought their tools, their food, and blankets to sleep on. Most stayed with their neighbors. Others lived in tents. They were all invited to family meals.

TOUGH GAMES

Pioneers worked hard—and played hard. For fun, men held knife-throwing, wrestling, and bare-knuckle boxing competitions.

This work party is beating the stems of flax plants. Then the flax will be spun into cloth.

The barn is finished. Now it is time to celebrate with music and dance!

Pioneers had work parties to pick apples, **husk** corn, chop logs, and sew quilts. When the work was done, they had a party inside a barn or outdoors! They filled a table with roasted lamb, hot bread, and delicious pies. Someone played a fiddle and everyone danced. Children drank lemonade. They were even allowed to stay up later than usual and to join in the fun.

Getting Food

Pioneers sometimes shot bears, moose, and deer. Many people worked together to drag a large animal home to eat.

Pioneer families kept several animals on the **homestead**. Cows provided milk. Chickens provided eggs. The families grew most of their other food. They grew corn, pumpkins, cabbage, beans, potatoes, and squash. They **pickled** some food to stop it from **spoiling**.

Pioneers hunted small animals in the nearby forests. Some used pet dogs to track wild animals. Squirrels, rabbits, ducks, and turkeys were roasted over a fire or added to a pot of soup. Sometimes children took fishing rods to the stream and brought back fish for supper. Pet cats kept rats, mice, and foxes away from fresh food.

SWEET FOOD

Sugar cost a lot of money at the **general store**. Pioneers sweetened their food with maple syrup or honey from bee hives.

Pioneers collected and boiled the **sap** from sugar maple trees to make maple syrup.

Cooking

The first pioneers cooked inside a fireplace. The fireplace was not very safe. As the mother cooked, her dress often caught on fire. Sometimes the food dropped into the fire. Later, people cooked on stoves. The food was on top and the fire was inside.

This woman is cooking on a wood-burning stove.

Pioneer Recipe—Corn Bread

Pioneers learned to make corn bread from the Native Americans. Some people spread butter or syrup on their corn bread. Follow the instructions below to make corn bread as the pioneers on **homesteads** did.

WARNING: Do not cook anything unless there is an adult to help you. Always ask an adult to do the cutting and cooking on a hot stove.

YOU WILL NEED
3/4 cup (180 g) corn meal
1 1/4 cup (310 g) flour
1/2 teaspoon salt
2 teaspoons baking powder
1/4 cup (60 g) sugar
1 egg
1 cup (240 ml) milk
1/4 cup (60 ml) vegetable oil, plus 1 tablespoon to grease the pan

FOLLOW THE STEPS

1. Preheat the oven to 400 degrees Farenheit (205 degrees Centigrade).
2. Use a paper towel to thinly spread 1 tablespoon of oil on the bottom of a square cake pan.

3. Stir together the corn meal, flour, salt, baking powder, and sugar.
4. Stir in the milk, egg, and 1/4 cup of oil.
5. When the batter is mixed but still lumpy, pour or scoop it out into the cake pan.

6. Bake for 20 to 25 minutes. You can tell if the bread is done by sticking a toothpick in the middle of the pan and removing it. If no batter sticks to the toothpick, the bread is done.

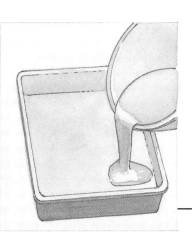

Growing into Towns

As more pioneers arrived, people built stores, schools, and churches. They built a bank, a doctor's office, and a post office. By the time the pioneer children grew up, they were living in a real town. Some of these people decided the town was too crowded. They moved farther west to Oregon and California.

The first towns had buildings made of wood. Later, buildings were made of brick with **slate** roofs. Wooden sidewalks were made on the main streets so people did not get their shoes and clothes muddy when it rained.

Glossary

apron clothing worn over a dress to keep it clean

arithmetic using numbers to add, subtract, multiply, and divide

cabin simple, small house built of wood

canvas thick material usually made from cotton

crops plants grown to provide food

Cumberland Gap path through the Appalachian Mountains near where Kentucky, Tennessee, and Virginia meet.

dunce cap tall, pointed cap given to students to wear who broke the rules

general store place that sold everything from clothes to food. Often it was the only store in town.

homestead house and surrounding open land used for farming

husk outer covering of corn; to remove the outer covering of corn

loft space just below the roof of a cabin

loom wooden frame for weaving threads or yarn into cloth

notch V-shaped cut

pickle to place food in a liquid such as salt water or vinegar to stop it from spoiling or rotting

sap liquid that flows through a plant

shear to cut the fleece, or wool coat, off a sheep

shelter covered place to protect people or animals

slate thin slice of rock used as a roof tile or as a writing surface

spoil to become rotten

well deep hole in the ground from which people get water

More Books to Read

Greenwood, Barbara *A Pioneer Sampler: The Daily Life of a Pioneer Family in 1840*. New York: Ticknor & Fields, 1995.

Knight, Theodore *The Pioneer Woman*. Vero Beach, Fla.: Rourke Book Company, 1994.

Index